FIGHTING
FROM
DARKNESS

Jaylen,
You are amazing, talented,
smart, and beautiful.
Never give up on your
goals and dreams.

Love,

Fighting from Darkness: How Long Will You Color Greatness

ISBN 978-0-578-51937-1

Copyright © 2019 by Lenora Lassiter. All rights reserved.

Published by Noahs Ark Publishing Service
www.noahsarkpublishing.com

Edited by Lisa Beasley
Graphic Design by Jamar Hargrove, NeedGFX; Teddy Wright
Author Photo by Benjamin Vilchez, Beauty of Life Photography

FIGHTING
FROM
DARKNESS

HOW LONG WILL YOU COLOR GREATNESS

Lenora Lassiter

Noahs Ark Publishing Service
Beverly Hills, California

This book is dedicated to my mother, Queen E. Dawson. You are the epitome of a strong woman, and you are a giver at heart. Thank you for giving me life and for being there when I needed you. For as long as I live, I will cherish our walks on the nature trail and our late-night talks. One day you shared with me that you wanted to take a typing class, and you didn't have the money to take it. You also shared that you were picked on while growing up, and many did not think you were going to achieve anything in life. Well, you did! Even though you never received a formal four-year degree, God has bestowed upon you an unequivocal amount of wisdom and wit. Just know that your baby girl loves you to pieces. You are my shining star, and I love you, momma! I am dedicating this book to you because I'm a reflection of you—a beautiful black queen.

CONTENTS

Acknowledgements ix

Introduction 1

Chapter 1
Colored My Esteem 5

Chapter 2
I'm Not Pretty 21

Chapter 3
Being Dark Felt Like a Curse 31

Chapter 4
When the Fights Began 37

Chapter 5
Humiliation 45

Chapter 6
God Made Me Dark 51

Chapter 7
Greatness Has No Color 59

Notes 69

ACKNOWLEDGEMENTS

I am grateful to God for allowing me to write this book. I would like to acknowledge my husband, Harold L. Lassiter, for supporting me in this endeavor. I would also like to acknowledge my father, Leo F. Dawson, Sr.; The Dawson Clan: Sherry Dawson-Williams, Leo F. Dawson, Jr., Isaac A. Dawson, and Joshua Dawson; all in my family who have made an impact in my life; and my late grandmothers, Catherine Wright and Ruby Dawson. Thank you, Laval Belle, for inspiring me to write this book.

INTRODUCTION

Fighting from Darkness: How Long Will You Color Greatness takes you on a vivid journey into a tumultuous time in my life—a time filled with bullying, fights, and humiliation, all because of the darkness of my skin. The experience caused me to question my very existence. If you haven't experienced bullying, it's an awful feeling that one never forgets. I decided to share my story because color discrimination and bullying are so prevalent in the lives of so many today. According to Riverside Medical Clinic Charitable Foundation, 1 in 7 students in grades K-12 are either a bully or have been a victim of bullying. An estimated 160,000 U.S. children miss school every day due to fear of being attacked or intimidated by other students. Eighty three percent of girls and 79 percent of boys report experiencing harassment. Six out of 10 teenagers say they witness bullying in school once a day.[1]

Bullying is a discussion that we need to have and is an epidemic that needs to be addressed. According to stopbullying.gov, kids who are bullied can experience negative physical, school, and mental health issues. Kids who are bullied are more likely to experience depression and anxiety, increased feelings of sadness and loneliness, changes in sleep and eating patterns, and loss of interest in activities they used to enjoy. These issues oftentimes transition into a child's adult years. Still there are other children who are victimized through bullying and can be at risk for committing suicide.[2]

Color discrimination, also known as colorism, is another major topic that needs to be addressed. Colorism not only exists in the African-American culture, but it also exists in many other communities of color. Being a victim of colorism also caused me to question my existence while growing up. That led me to often ask the question: "Who said black is beautiful?" The suffering I went through as a dark-skinned child taught me that black is beautiful only if a person is a certain shade of black.

At the age of 7 years old, being a dark-skinned little girl who was trying to figure out life seemed more like a curse than a blessing. Subsequently, black was not beautiful to me. At that age, my main concern should have been learning how to write my name in cursive and perfecting my reading comprehension and math skills. Instead, I was more concerned about why God had made me so dark and why I was being treated differently. I dreaded going to school because I knew I was going to be bullied on the school bus while on the way to school, in my classes during school, and on the bus on the way home from school.

I was also ridiculed for the way I dressed, but being bullied because of the color of my skin opened a river of emotions that flowed from my childhood to adulthood. I did not have a say in my complexion or the family I was born into, but I was picked on as if I could choose to wash the blackness off my skin. This entire experience affected my self-esteem and skewed my perception of beauty.

Being bullied took me through a range of emotions, and at one point, I wanted to die. But one day it finally hit me: I could never change the color of my skin. I finally embraced the true beauty of it. Now, I love everything about the darkness of my skin.

You may ask yourself, "Why should I even turn to the next page to start reading this book? Is it worth my time?" I can say it is worth it. You may not have ever experienced anything like what I have experienced before. But I guarantee you there is someone in your family or among your acquaintances that is dealing with this issue. If you are an educator, you may have a student who is struggling with insecurity. If you are a parent, you may have a child that is dealing with feelings of rejection. If you are a mentor, you may be mentoring someone who is dealing with hopelessness. These are real issues, and if left unattended, they could lead to even greater problems.

Whether it's you or someone you know, it is my hope that this book will help people in meaningful and impactful ways. The path to healing may not be an easy one, and it may take some time, but it will come. It is my prayer that this book is one of the tools that can be used to overcome the darkness that attempts to steal self-esteem and self-worth so that we can change the culture and the conversation. And I pray most of all that those who read this book can arrive at and discover their greatness and full potential, knowing that greatness is not determined by color but by what lies within.

CHAPTER 1

COLORED MY ESTEEM

My name is Lenora Marie Dawson Lassiter, but I was born
Lenora Marie Dawson. I was born in Fayetteville, North Carolina, during one of the best months of the year–October. I am
one of five children and the second oldest. My sister, Sherry, is
the oldest. She is the second momma to all of us and is protective
of all her siblings. If you have an older sibling, I am sure you can
relate to what I'm saying. We are also three years apart, but we
have twin spirits. She is one of my greatest supporters and cheer-
leaders. We were also roommates until we married. We married
our spouses six months apart. My sister is the best sister in the
world. She has seen me at my lowest and seen me at my highest.

I also have three brothers: Leo Jr., Isaac, and Joshua. Leo
Jr. and I are sixteen months apart, so as you can tell, my parents
did not waste any time bringing their first son into the world. My
mom calls him June, but I thought he would be called Junior,
since he was named after my dad. As a child, Leo was very inquis-
itive and started removing door knobs at the age of 5 years old.
As an adult, he is good with his hands and can fix a lot of things.
Isaac was the knee baby. *Knee baby* is a term that is used in African-American families. The knee baby is slightly older than the
youngest child. Isaac was an athlete in school and was the child
that I still say, to this day, is my mom's favorite child.

Joshua is the baby boy. I call him my parent's oopsie baby
because my mom had him at 40 years old. My dad always wanted
a large family, and he told my mom that he wanted seven children.

But my mom said that she was not going to be barefoot and pregnant all her life. After Joshua, the oven was turned off, never to be turned back on again.

My parents told me that, when I was a baby, there was a time when they were running low on milk. One day, an eighteen-wheeler came to our home, and the driver told them that he had a delivery for them. When they asked what the delivery was, the driver immediately told them that the delivery was a truckload of baby milk formula. My parents said they did not have to buy baby milk for me for several months. And to this day, they do not know who sent the delivery.

I guess that is the reason why I loved milk so much as a child. I drank milk with everything. Late one night, my mom caught me in the kitchen eating a hotdog and drinking milk. They should have given me the nickname Milky. (In the African-American community, parents are known for giving their children nicknames.) If I had a bologna sandwich, I had to have a glass of milk. Oh, and not to mention, I loved dunking my cookies in milk. I would drop an entire cookie in the milk and then pull it out and eat it. But today, I really do not drink milk. However, I do drink almond milk, but only in cereal.

I grew up on Brookwood Avenue. My neighborhood was mixed with both African-American and Caucasian people. Some of our neighbors were awesome, and some were not. Mr. and Mrs. McDonald were awesome. They would let us come to their house after school when my parents were not home. They had a den, where they had a pool table. My siblings and I loved to spend time in their den, because we loved to play pool. We really did not understand how to play pool at that time, but we would try to get the balls in the hole. On Sundays, Mrs. McDonald's house was packed. All her adult children and their children would come

over for Sunday dinner. Her family members' cars would line the
street. A few times, my dad had to ask them to move their cars,
because they were blocking our driveway.

Mr. and Mrs. McDonald had an older granddaughter that
stayed with them for a little while. Their granddaughter had a son
named DJ. DJ became one of our childhood friends. He would
often come over to our house to play. We'd play basketball and
kickball. But, after DJ and his mom moved out and Mrs. McDonald died, we lost touch with him.

Our other next-door neighbors were a Caucasian older couple.
They lived beside my parents for a few years and then moved out.
I really didn't get a chance to know them. The only thing I can
remember about them is that they kept a well-manicured lawn.
After they moved out, Ms. Betty, her husband, and her son, Bobby,
moved in. They were a nice family. However, I got a whipping
because of Bobby. Ms. Gladys, another one of our neighbors
who lived down the street, told my mom that I was on the side
of the house with Bobby, "being fast." But we were just talking.
However, my mom believed Ms. Gladys, and I got a spanking that
I will never forget. Just know that the spanking took place in the
living room, not far from the front door.

We also had another couple in our neighborhood that caused
trouble. Their names were Leslie and Carl. They were also white.
Leslie and Carl had two daughters, Tina and Lena. Leslie accused
my sister, brothers, and me of picking on her daughter at the
bus stop, and she started recording us whenever we were at the
bus stop. She would yell at us and then call the school, making
false accusations about us picking on her daughter. Since Leslie
kept complaining to the school, the principal rode the bus home
one day to see if the accusations were true, and of course, they
were not. Leslie eventually warmed up to us as we got older. She

finally realized that we were not going to move anywhere, and they weren't moving anywhere, so we needed to get along. In junior high and part of high school, we did not have a computer at home, so Leslie would allow us to use her computer to write reports and do research for school projects.

Another one of our neighbors was a lady we called Ms. Jennette, who had two daughters. One day I saw her working in her yard, planting flowers, so I said hello and asked her if she would like to buy something for my school fundraiser. She looked at me and told me to get out of her yard. I never set foot in her yard again.

There was also this older lady named Ms. Geraldine. Ms. Geraldine lived alone and was an old and bitter woman. Every time I saw her, she had on her gown, with socks and slippers. She would sweep her porch in her gown, take out the trash in her gown, and stand on her porch smoking a cigarette in her gown. Ms. Geraldine had Siamese cats who sat in her front window as if they were her personal bodyguards. She did not want any of the neighborhood children in her yard. When we played ball with our friends, she would say, "Stay out my yard. Don't let that ball come in my yard again." If the ball ended up in her yard, we would be afraid to go get it because she would scold us.

But then there were nice people in our neighborhood, like Mr. Holsten, who was single and a preacher. He would always encourage the children in the community by supporting our school fundraisers and always having something positive to say to the neighborhood kids.

Oh! And I cannot forget Mr. and Mrs. China. They were an elderly couple who lived at the end of the street, and they were as sweet as pie. They had a granddaughter named Monique, who taught my sister and me how to play the piano. My sister continued to take lessons for quite some time, but I stopped. I really did not have an interest in playing.

My parents, Leo Sr. and Queen, have been married for over forty years. They were very pious and strict when I was younger. They also were ministers. We lived and breathed church. As a young child, I can remember my mom and dad getting us up early for church and loading us into the car and driving to Roseboro, North Carolina, to New Galilee Holiness Church. The pastor's name was Pastor Walker. We would stay in church until two o'clock in the afternoon almost every Sunday. After church, we would eat at a member's house and then go back to church at four o'clock. I must admit, New Galilee Church members were some of the best cooks ever. They had the best snap and field peas I've ever tasted.

I remember one of the deacons giving us some Circus Peanuts candy if we behaved well, and I also remember getting peppermints and cinnamon candy from some of the church mothers. I could tell that some of that candy had been in their purses for a long time, because the candy was chewable. Hard candy is not supposed to be chewable. It is only chewable if it is old. It was old, but it was good. I was about 6 years old during that time, but I can remember falling asleep in church. My mom would wake me up and tell me to pay attention. I was not interested in paying attention; I was tired and hungry. We very seldom got to eat breakfast prior to going to church because my parents believed that we needed to fast. I've always wondered if other people's children were able to eat before going to church.

New Galilee had some nice people and some mean people. There was an older lady at New Galilee that I remember being afraid of. Her name was Mother Bee. Mother Bee sat near the choir stand and played the piano and looked mean. She always had a mean look on her face. She also had a little mustache. I never asked my parents about her mustache because I did not want to get in trouble. Years later, Mother Bee passed away. I am not sure what happened to her. But there was another older lady named Mother Faison. Unlike Mother Bee, Mother Faison was nice. She was kind to my siblings and me and often invited us over for food.

We drove back and forth between Roseboro, North Carolina, and Garland, North Carolina, for several years, and then my parents started attending a church in Fayetteville, North Carolina, called Elizabeth Chapel, pastored by Elizabeth Cole. My dad told us that Pastor Cole had helped him during his initial stages of learning about Christianity. She also allowed him to stay with her and her husband for a short period of time. That was nice of her to do that, but if you asked me, she was mean. She was short and feisty. I can remember her preaching. She would stop in the middle of her sermon and tell parents to wake their children up. I was one of those children that fell asleep when she was preaching, because the service was too long, and it seemed as if she fussed the entire sermon. If Pastor Cole saw someone chewing gum in church, she would tell that person to take the gum out of their mouth. This was new for me. I'd never seen a preacher stop in the middle of his or her sermon and call people out. Her husband was a deacon named Alexander Cole. He was a nice man, but I must be honest. I don't see how he put up with her. In my opinion, she bossed him around.

Another reason why I did not like going to Elizabeth Chapel was because some of the kids that attended the church were mean and would pick on my sister and me. I remember that, usually, after service was over, my sister and brothers and I would walk toward our car, preparing to leave. But we had to wait on our parents. Some of the other church kids who were older than we were would hang around in the parking lot, snickering and laughing at us.

While at Elizabeth Chapel, my siblings and I sang in the children's choir, but we seldom got a chance to lead any songs. There was only a select few who felt they were capable enough to lead songs. I was just over it all. My parents finally left Elizabeth Chapel and went to Clinton Chapel, where the pastor was Willie Burch.

My parents actually knew Pastor Burch before he became a pastor. One day they were riding around in downtown Fayetteville, and they saw Mr. Burch sitting on the steps of the library. They started talking to him about Jesus. He told my parents that he had been sitting there thinking about which bank he was going to rob. My parents invited him to come sit in their car, and they continued their conversation about Jesus. Mr. Burch accepted Jesus into his life in the back seat of my parent's car that day.

Clinton Chapel was okay, but there were mean people there too. I'd never seen so many people who claimed to be Christians and yet acted so mean. They would get up during testimony service and start testifying and would start throwing off on each other (meaning that when a person was supposed to be testifying about God's goodness in his or her life and what HE has done, instead, that person would use the opportunity to talk about a person without saying the person's name). It would be better known today as throwing shade. Even though I was a child, I knew when people were throwing off on someone else. But one good thing about going to Clinton Chapel was that Pastor Burch's children were nice. My sister, brothers, and I had a great relationship with all his children, Alicia, Willie Jr., Emanuel, and Jacob. Pastor Burch's wife was nice too!

I saw so much as a child in church. There was this older lady named Mother Cole, who had just finished testifying and then sat down on the pew and broke it. Some of the deacons rushed over to help her. She was a heavy-set woman. I dared not laugh, because I knew I would get in trouble.

After attending Clinton Chapel for a while, my parents started pastoring, in 1991.

Our home became an inn and a counseling center. There were times when people needed somewhere to stay, and they would stay with us for a short period of time. We would have to give up our beds and make pallets on the floor. Our home was not that big. We only had three bedrooms and one bath, but we made it work.

Our living room became a place of healing and prayer. People would come and pour out their problems to our parents. When they came to our house, my siblings and I had to go in our room and close the door or go outside and play. I was that child that wanted to know what was going on. So, of course, I would find every excuse to go into the kitchen. I would go get water and look for snacks. And I despised staying inside our room because we did not have cable when we were younger. We had a TV with an antenna. The antenna didn't work well, so my sister would put a clothes hanger inside the antenna to help get a better signal. If that TV could talk, it would tell you how many times we slapped the side of it, trying to get the picture to come in clear.

During my parent's living room sessions, they would pray for people. Some of the people were delivered from evil spirits. After they left, my parents would open the doors to the home and pray again to make sure the evil spirits did not linger. They firmly believed that evil spirits could attach to other people.

As a preacher's kid (PK), I saw my parents go through so much. They were mistreated, used, and lied on. There were times when my parents would go through their freezer and pantries to feed people and give them money. We saw people come and go in ministry. One Sunday, when we were getting ready to leave the house for church, my dad went outside and discovered that someone had sliced the tires on all our cars and the church van. We knew it was one of the members who was upset with my dad and had recently left the church. At a young age, I learned that I could not trust many people, and I still do not to this day.

I've seen my parents sacrifice so much to help people. Gladys, a neighbor from down the street, had three kids. When my parents bought things for us, they also made sure her kids had something too. When my dad bought us bikes for Christmas, he bought them bikes for Christmas. Gladys' children and my siblings and I were like family. We ate together, climbed trees together, and fussed, fought, and sang together. We were good friends until their mom got married and moved to Michigan. Years later, her husband died, and Gladys moved back to North Carolina. One of her children stayed in Michigan, and one of them got married and moved to Alabama. After returning to North Carolina, Gladys' oldest son, Maurice, died, which was devastating.

If you asked my parents, they would tell you that I never really caused them any heartache or issues as a child. At the age of seven, I was a lovable and sweet child, and I loved both of my parents dearly. My dad taught me how to save money and work hard for what I want in life. He also taught me to be independent. He showed me that a man is supposed to be a protector and provider for his family, and he always taught me the importance of maintaining good credit. He would always tell us, "Do not mess your credit up because I am not co-signing for anything." My dad had to learn how to be a father while being a father, because his father died when he was only 13 years old. So, he had a lot to learn, being a father to five children.

My mother, Queen Esther, and I have always shared a special bond. She is a wise woman with a strong gift of discernment. She taught me about the importance of wisdom and how to be frugal, how to negotiate, and how to be independent. She also taught me about the importance of keeping my virginity until marriage. I always wanted to follow my mother around as a little girl. There were days when I would hear my parents talking about going somewhere, and I knew, if I asked, my father would tell me I couldn't go. But I always wanted to be with my mother. There were times when I would get in our station wagon before they could get outside and curl up on the floor behind the driver's seat so they would not see me. Once we were at least a good distance from home, I would pop up, and they would say, "What are you doing back there?" But they were too far away from home, and gas was scarce, so I knew they were not going to turn around and take me home.

I didn't like staying home much because my brothers Leo and Isaac would often get in a fight, and my sister would have to break them up. Oftentimes, my parents would be away helping someone, and they would have to come back home because my brothers were fighting. I am so glad those days are over. We are a close-knit family now.

We took a few family vacations when my siblings and I were children, but most of them were centered around something dealing with church. I can remember going to Canada, New York, New Jersey, Pennsylvania, Georgia, and South Carolina. We spent so much time in South Carolina that I thought we were going to pick up the Geechee accent. We often visited Moncks Corner, Huger, and Timmonsville, South Carolina.

As a child, I was in church every Sunday, either singing or ushering. On Saturdays my parents often went shopping to buy school and church clothes for us. They didn't shop at average stores, like Sears or JCPenney. They shopped at the Y.S. Store. Y.S. stood for yard sales. So, for most of our childhood, my siblings and I wore hand-me-downs. But my mom and dad always made sure we looked decent. My parents did not have a lot of money. The only things we were able to buy new was a pair of Sunday shoes and school shoes. My Sunday shoes were patent leather, and when they started to get dull, my mom would put Vaseline on them. I hated that because, when I walked on dirt, the Vaseline was like a magnetic force that attracted the dirt to my shoes.

I was brought up Pentecostal and wore either a skirt or dress to school every day. I also wore a pair of white Keds shoes, better known as bobos. When my shoes got dirty, I would wash them in the washing machine and put them on the porch to dry. Sometimes, when they were not dry enough, I would put them in the oven, because we did not have a dryer during my early childhood. My Keds could only go through so many washes. And when they did, I would attempt to use white shoe polish on them. Long jean skirts and sneakers was the worst style combination ever created within the Pentecostal church.

On Saturday afternoons, my parents would summon my siblings and me to the living room and tell us to get ready to go to the rest home (which we refer to today as a nursing home) later that evening. We'd go there to sing and read the Bible to the residents. I was a little afraid of some of the people because they would have outbursts and wanted to hug us. I was young, and this was new to me, but I finally got accustomed to it. My siblings and I were involved in doing community service and working at a young age.

My dad worked full-time, and my mom stayed home to raise us. However, my mom did do a few odds-and-ends jobs. She cleaned houses and delivered newspapers and magazines. When my siblings and I were in our preteen years, we helped her deliver newspapers during the summer. She would have to go to the *Fayetteville Observer* and pick up a stack of papers. We would sit in our living room, roll the papers up, and put them in plastic sleeves. Then we'd load them in her station wagon for delivery. I used to hate delivering those papers because we couldn't just throw them in the yards. We had to hang them on a door or fence. Some of the deliveries were in neighborhoods where kids lived that I knew, and I did not want them to see me delivering newspapers in my mom's big, brown station wagon. That car was ugly. When we delivered newspapers in neighborhoods where my classmates lived, I would quickly duck and beg my mom not to send me to certain houses. But, despite it all, my mom was generous, and she paid us well.

My sister and brothers were the first version of friends I had. We did everything together, from making mud pies to playing battleship, stick ball, and monopoly. At the age of seven, I only had a few friends in school. Most of the other kids were mean to me and would constantly call me names because of my dark skin. They would say, "Hey, darky" or "Why you so black?" I really did not know how to respond because I was so young, so I would just roll my eyes. I never told my mom and dad about being called degrading names. I kept it to myself. I couldn't wait until it was time to leave school each day. My teacher would walk us from the pod (classroom area) to the bus. I couldn't wait for the bus to pull off from Belvedere Avenue. As I rode the school bus home from

Margaret Willis Elementary School, I would always wonder why I was picked on for being dark and why I was so dark.

The sad part about the situation is that the name calling was not coming from the white children, but from the black children. I could never understand why people from the same ethnicity as I were so mean to me! Why? As I previously stated, I never had a conversation with my parents at this age because I was still trying to figure it out. Yes, at 7 years old, I was trying to figure out why this was happening to me. No child should have to endure that type of verbal abuse. At that age, I should have been enjoying being a child, not trying to figure out why I was this color or trying to figure out what to say when someone started bullying me because of my dark skin.

There was this little boy named Maurice, who I guess zoned in on the fact that I was a loner and that I needed some sort of validation. So he started talking to me, but within a few weeks, I became a victim of his name-calling. "Hey, Blacky" was the salutation he greeted me with. Feeling inferior and being called names was painful. And to add to the dehumanizing feelings I experienced were the giggles of some of my classmates who laughed at Maurice's comments about me. One other classmate I remember vividly was Nigel. Both of these little guys were much lighter than I was, and they picked on me often.

I often wondered why I couldn't be the color of my sister. She was brown-skinned, and to my knowledge, she did not suffer being taunted by children every single day. I wanted to be lighter, and I couldn't come to grips with my dark complexion. I just felt worthless, trying to figure out *why me?* Why was I this dark-skinned girl? In addition to being dark-skinned, I also suffered with eczema, a skin disease that exacerbated my complexion and caused hyperpigmentation all over my body, especially on my hands, arms, legs, and feet. To be honest, I just felt ugly, and I believed I would never fit in anywhere.

Being taunted daily affected my self-esteem and my self-worth. If I could have found a pencil and erased my dark pigmentation, I would have. Looking back, I am surprised that I was able to focus on my studies at such a tender age, but I guess I had an innate willpower to persevere in my studies. I also believe that certain teachers, such as Mrs. Corn, Mrs. Broom, Ms. Powell, Mrs. Wright, and Mrs. Paige, pushed me to be a great student, not knowing what I was facing on a daily basis.

Being scarred this early in life had me thinking about my future as a young girl. My esteem was colored. I said to myself, "When I grow up, I do not want to marry a dark-skinned man. He must be light-skinned because I do not want to have dark-skinned children." I did not want my children to experience the pain that I was going through growing up as a dark-skinned girl. I had made up my mind that my child was not going to be a victim of my decision to marry a man with dark skin. My child would not be targeted, ostracized, and marginalized because of the color of his or her skin.

CHAPTER 2

I'M NOT PRETTY

My self-esteem was colored at a young age, and that infiltrated my belief about beauty, love, and acceptance. Having beauty, love, and acceptance equated with being light-skinned. I literally felt that I was not pretty or even attractive because of my dark skin. After leaving Margaret Willis Elementary School, I attended Edgewood Elementary School. Edgewood Elementary housed grades four through six. Edgewood equaled puberty, and everyone was smelling themselves, as the old folks used to say. Edgewood was the first place where I was introduced to the terms "boyfriend" and "girlfriend." And I also became aware of the different brands of clothes and shoes that were out during that time. Some of the kids were outfitted in Nike, Adidas, and Jordans. I wore no-name clothes.

A lot of the girls were in competition to attract the attention of Willie, Tyrone, and Shaun. I also started to notice that all the boys wanted to date only the light-skinned girls, or girls who were not dark-skinned. This reinforced my belief that being dark-skinned was not beautiful at all. And battling eczema only made things worse. I would have rashes all over my body. At night I would scratch so badly that my bed linen would have blood on it. My mom would come in my room at night to keep me from scratching my skin, but as soon as she left, I would start scratching again. The itching was severe, and I just wanted relief. The only remedy, for me, was to scratch, but each time I scratched, I was causing my skin to break, bleed, and darken.

My parents would take me to the doctor, and the doctor would prescribe creams. But the creams did not help. I remember my parents taking me to Dr. Sherriff. He was an older Caucasian doctor. He would tell my parents that he, along with other physicians, did not know what caused eczema and that the only thing he could do was prescribe creams to help with the itching. I tried everything. I even did Clorox baths. When I got out of the tub, I could see my skin floating in the bath water. The Clorox baths helped a little, but then I smelled like bleach.

My parents once told me that people used to tell them that, if they didn't get some help for me, someone was going to turn them in to Social Services for child neglect. Now, how ignorant was that? My parents were doing all they could to alleviate the pain I was experiencing. It hurt them to know that I was being plagued by this skin disease, and there was nothing they could do about it.

One day my parents went on a trip to Washington, D.C. They left my sister, brothers, and me with this older lady who lived in Grove View Terrace. While keeping us, she noticed how I was itching. She saw that I would not stop scratching, so she went to get something out of her medicine cabinet to put on my skin. In African-American communities, the older generations always had a remedy for everything, and if a person was sick or in pain, they would go to their medicine cabinet or kitchen to find something to help or heal the person of what ailed them.

Despite my sister's protests and warning not to put anything on my skin, the lady paid her no mind and started applying the liquid on my skin anyway. We later discovered that it was sulfur. I started to have an allergic reaction almost immediately. My skin started to burn and itch even more. My sister shouted, "I told you not to put that on my sister's skin. She has sensitive skin." Not only did my skin break out even more, but it also turned extremely dark. When my parents arrived the next day to pick us up, they could not believe what they saw. My skin was a wreck. My mom and dad asked the lady what happened, and my sister blurted out, "She put something on Lenora's skin. I told her not to put it on her, but she didn't listen to me." My parents felt bad about this happening to me, but the damage had already been done. The only thing they could do was apply cold compresses to my skin to help with the burning and itching. My parents never left us with her again.

So, when I went back to school, the dark jokes continued. I really did not understand why I was battling so much at a young age. I was very embarrassed about my skin, and I was uncomfortable talking about it. One day, as I was standing outside talking to my next-door neighbor, she asked me what was wrong with my hands (why did they look like they did). I told her they were gloves that were part of my Halloween outfit. I didn't know what else to say. I didn't even have a Halloween outfit, because my parents did not allow us to celebrate Halloween. Although my neighbor meant no harm, I was young, and I didn't want her to know what was going on with me.

Now, as I sit, reflect, and write this book, I realize that my eczema was exacerbated because of stress. I can remember taking a brown paper towel and using it as a wrap for my right hand because my hand was oozing with pus, and it would be so difficult to write because certain parts of my skin were broken. In addition to all of that, the pus had a certain stench to it. One day it was so bad that I had to ask my friend Renada to write for me because I could barely hold the pencil in my hand. My hand was swollen and in extreme pain. Because of this, I was often unhappy. I wanted to know why God would make one color more beautiful than another, and why was I afflicted with this skin disease? Why would HE do such a thing? As a child, it was so hard for me to understand. My only concern in life back then should have been with making memories, but some of my memories were not so good. Sometimes I would just sit in my room and cry. My sister would tell my momma I was crying. My mom always thought I was crying because of the eczema, but I was actually crying for two reasons—dealing with eczema and being bullied because of my dark skin.

I tried to fit in with some of the popular, pretty girls, but I was not accepted into the pretty girls' clique. I was a loner and had only one to two friends. It seemed to me that my skin complexion stuck out like a magnet, attracting black jokes. Despite the memories of constant ridicule, I do remember my librarian, Ms. Thomas. She was a petite African-American lady who wore glasses. She was a positive role model in my life, and she showed me love, which made me feel a little better. She would allow me to assist her with organizing books in the library. I saw Ms. Thomas recently, and I was glad to see that she still has a pleasant smile and encouraging words to say. I also remember my teacher Ms. Wilborne. She was Caucasian, but she loved all her students. She showed me love and even took me for a ride in her red sports car after school. She was one of my favorite teachers at Edgewood. The love that Ms. Wilborne showed me (and her other students) was unconditional. Her kindness shown toward me gave me a little sense of pride, but it did not help validate my beauty. I still believed that I was not pretty.

After finishing the sixth grade at Edgewood Elementary School, I then attended Reid Ross Junior High School, and the black jokes continued. Reid Ross was a predominantly African-American School. Nathan reminded me that I was not pretty each time I walked into Mr. Swann's algebra class. Mr. Swann was an African-American heavy-set teacher who wore his shirt tucked in his pants and wore big, black glasses. When he taught, he would smack periodically while talking. He sat on a stool most of the class time. He would say, "Alright, class, open your books to page 45." Then he would pull out his blue dry-erase marker and start writing algebraic expressions on the overhead projector. He was, and still is, the pastor of Second Missionary Baptist Church in Fayetteville, North Carolina. I could tell he was a preacher just by the way he articulated certain things and the way he said, "Alright, class." He would sometimes say, "Now, now. 2 x 3 equals..." and then would call on someone to explain it. I sometimes wish he would have called on Nathan to solve the problems, since he enjoyed calling people out and picking on them.

Nathan was an African-American guy that not too many people messed with. He lived on Preston Avenue, and no one really messed with or dared to challenge anyone from Preston Avenue. Preston was known for drugs and violence. So who would say something back to a guy who lived on Preston? I will answer that—very few. Nathan knew that he could bully me because he knew that I wouldn't do anything. In algebra class, he would say out loud, "Look who's coming to dinner: Blacky Ella." Then some of the students in the class would start laughing. I really didn't think his jokes were funny, but he made it a point to get some laughs from some of our peers by calling me names.

I hated going to that class. Defeat and anxiety washed over me whenever I thought about going. One day, I walked into class, and I didn't hear, "Look who's coming to dinner: Blacky Ella." So, I assumed Nathan was absent that day. But then he showed up just as the bell rang. He walked to his seat, which was in the back of the class, and said, "Girl, you look like Celie from the movie

The Color Purple. Then he asked another guy in class, "Don't she look like Celie?" This, of course, made some of my classmates burst out in laughter. Whenever Mr. Swann heard Nathan's jokes, he would look over his glasses and tell him to cut it out. I wished I'd had the guts to stand up to Nathan, but I didn't. I oftentimes wished I'd had an older brother or a male cousin that attended junior high with me who could have stood up to bullies like Nathan. Even though I was being bullied in junior high school, I never found the courage to tell my parents about it.

Since Nathan had started bullying me and joking on me, others started joining in on it. There were times when I would hear, "Hey, Blacky." "Look at that tar baby," "Black smut." "Hey, Celie." "Girl, you are ugly." One of the other black jokes that I remember is "Girl, you so black, people can't see you at night, so you will need to smile to show your teeth for people to see you." I couldn't wait to go home in the afternoons. I lived less than five minutes from Reid Ross Junior High, but the bus ride home seemed like hours because of the bullying I had to endure.

There was this boy named Tyree who was younger than I, but he would get on the bus and start calling me names and taunting me. Tyree was short and brown-skinned, with slanted eyes and acne on his face. No one messed with Tyree because he was Ricky and Randy's baby brother, and no one messed with them. When Tyree picked on me, there were things I could have said to him, but I didn't. He and his brothers were notorious for fighting. So, again, I had already lost the battle with him because he knew I wasn't going to do anything.

Then there was this other boy named Brandon. Brandon taunted me about my dark-skin too. He was known for picking on people. He would pick on two other girls on our bus who were sisters. He teased them about being dark-skinned and called them butches. One day, I was eating a bag of hot Cheetos on the way home from school. Brandon said, "Give me some chips, with your black self." "No," I replied. He then snatched them out of my hand and started eating them in my face. After he finished, he had the audacity to lick his fingers. I wanted to punch him in his face, but I couldn't do anything because he was much bigger than I was. He was so hateful.

Can you imagine trying to get an education while waking up every day wondering *who will start bullying me today?* It was a feeling like no other. I sometimes attempted to hang with some of the popular girls in school to seek protection, but again, I really did not fit in with anyone. I even had an older cousin who taught at the school. I said to myself *well, maybe if I tell them she is my cousin they will not mess with me.* But she told me not to tell anyone that we were related. I really didn't know why she told me that. But I honored her request.

Each year, around Valentine's Day, the school would have a Carnation Sale, which allowed guys to buy carnations for girls that they liked and vice versa. The carnations were beautiful. They were generally red, pink, and white. During the two years that I was at Reid Ross Junior High, I never received a carnation. I felt that I was not pretty enough to get one anyway. I must admit, my dad always made sure that my sister and I received something on Valentine's Day, and I was appreciative. But it was something about getting a carnation from someone at school. I was young, and there was a part of me that needed validation outside of my family.

Being bullied and feeling that I wasn't pretty caused me to think less of myself. It had gotten to the point where I wished I was dead so I wouldn't have to deal with it all. There was also a point where I thought about slitting my wrist. But I knew there was no forgiveness from God if I took my own life. My mom kept her knives in a brown knife holder, and I went as far as taking a knife out of the knife holder and literally allowing the ridges to press upon my skin. Tears were rolling down my face, and I just wanted the feelings of hurt and dejection to be over with. I sat there for a few minutes, but I knew it wasn't the right thing to do. And today I am here to tell the story. The bullying affected me, but it didn't kill me.

I often wished I was pretty, like the two Shannons and Dana, Latoya, and Johnetta, or I was tough, like Cametrius and Shameia. Shannon C. and Dana were popular and wore the latest jerseys with their tennis skirts. Cametrius and Shameia were both dark-skinned, but not too many people messed with them because they would fight. Plus, Shameia had a cousin named Mareda, and no one really messed with her either.

I would always look at my sister and say, "My sister is pretty. Why couldn't I have been born with a beautiful complexion?" I would say to myself, "Why didn't I take after my father, who has brown-skin, versus my mom, who has dark skin?" I was young and confused, and I couldn't appreciate the generous dosage of melanin that God had bestowed upon me. My views of what pretty looked like was distorted due to the bullying I suffered. Sometimes I would stare at other girls, dreaming of being lighter than I was. Being lighter would have allowed me the opportunity to be viewed as pretty and accepted.

Not long ago, while my mom and I were walking on the nature trail in Clark Park, my mom told me that, as a teenager, she had wanted to bleach her skin. She said she had told one of her cousins about wanting to bleach her skin, and her cousin had recommended the type of bleaching cream she should buy. But she never went through with it. She went on to tell me how glad she was that she did not mess up her skin by attempting to use bleaching cream. I didn't follow-up that day and ask her why she had felt the need to bleach her skin, because we immediately jumped to another conversation. But a few weeks later, I did ask her. She told me that she did not want to be dark-skinned. When I asked her why, she replied, "I felt like, if I were lighter, I would have been prettier." I then said to myself, *"Wow, I felt the same thing too."* She went on to say that some of the older people in her neighborhood would see her and started saying, "There goes my pretty little black girl." And whenever she heard those words, it would make her feel good. After hearing those words, she said she no longer had the desire to bleach her skin. I never knew until that day that both my mom and I had once felt that we'd been prettier if we had lighter skin. It was a moment I will never forget. My mom and I both had come to realize that we were fearfully and wonderfully made—that we are beautiful in the skin that we were wrapped in at conception. We realized that our beauty is not based on the color of our skin but on the beauty that radiates from our personality and character. The darkness of our skin does not diminish the beauty that emanates from within us. If anything, it enhances it. We had learned to embrace and appreciate our beautiful dark skin as much as we appreciated all the other attributes God has given us. That moment was special because I realized that, despite our past, we were no longer deceived. We knew that we were beautiful, and no one could make us believe anything different.

CHAPTER 3

BEING DARK FELT LIKE A CURSE

As a dark-skinned girl, I felt like I was cursed—cursed in a sense of misfortune. I could not understand why I was being bullied because of the color of my skin. I felt that no one would ever find me attractive, and I would never be married. I felt I was destined to be alone and unwanted. The opposite of a curse is a blessing, and I sure didn't feel like a blessing. I believe that it was because I was dark-skinned that I did not have many friends and that not many people wanted to hang around me. My skin color, coupled with my Pentecostal attire, seemed to be a plague that no one wanted to catch.

I often thought about how my life would have been easier if I had been lighter. Light-skinned people were viewed as prettier. Whenever I watched TV, I seldom saw a dark-skinned woman depicted as the main character or the person that the guy was attracted to. During slavery, the light-skinned slaves worked in the house and were viewed as privileged, and the dark-skinned slaves worked in the fields in the hot sun. They were called field Negroes. I felt like a field Negro.

When I was in high school, my friend Chinyere came over to my house to work on a project for one of our classes. After we finished our project, I asked my mom if Chinyere and I could go to the carnival that was down the street from our house. My mom and sister went with us. I am not a fan of ferris wheels, nor do I like fast rides. But I wanted to get on a ride that night. As Chinyere and I were waiting to get on the ride, I noticed that the operator of the ride, an African-American male, was watching me. I asked him if the ride was fast, and he said it was not. Prior to getting on the ride, I said, "Sir, please do not go too fast with this ride." He made a smart remark, and I told him I was going to scream if he made the ride go too fast. Suddenly, he said, "You remind me of my ex-wife. She was dark-skinned and mean like you." I was shocked and confused. He went on to say, "All y'all dark-skinned women are mean." I was so baffled. This man did not know me. However, just because I was dark-skinned, he decided that I was mean. I felt belittled and was very upset.

But Chinyere and I decided that we were still going to get on the ride, and we did. The operator started the ride off slowly, and the ride remained that way for about five minutes. Then, out of nowhere, the operator did exactly what I had asked him not to do—he made the ride go extremely fast. My heart started racing, and I started breaking out in a sweat. I started screaming and feeling sick. My sister noticed, and she yelled, "Turn the ride off, so I can get my sister off. Turn it off." Once the ride came to a stop, my sister and Chinyere helped me off, and I went to the nearest trash can and threw up. The operator looked at me with a smirk on his face, as if he had gotten vengeance against his ex-wife. It was one of the weirdest experiences I've ever had. I had been punished by a man I did not know, just because I was dark-skinned and his wife was dark-skinned. It was absurd. I never really cared too much for getting on rides that go a certain speed, but that experience has deterred me from theme parks ever since. I haven't been on another ride since then. If I go to a theme park, I only go on rides that go super slow, maybe a slide, and that's about it.

The carnival ride experience replayed in my head often, especially when I used to hear people in conversation say that dark-skinned girls are mean and have an attitude problem. Why are we given such stigmas? Why are such negative generalizations made about us? Every time I would hear such ignorant comments, my skin would cringe, and I'd wonder how people could be so ignorant and make such frivolous comments.

When we finally got a computer in our home, I would go on AOL.com and read the Black Voices section. I would read relationship threads, and to my amazement, I would read comments like "black man seeking black woman." I would scroll down on the thread and read "black woman must be light-skinned with long hair, or brown-skinned with medium-length hair." No one wanted the dark-skinned women. I would even read articles that indicated that rappers and R&B singers wanted only light-skinned video vixens featured in their videos, which confirmed my belief that being dark-skinned was a curse.

Growing up in church, I noticed that most guys who came to church would be attracted to the preacher's daughters. Well, most guys were attracted to my sister, but not to me. They did not think I was pretty. And what really made me angry was when my sister did not want to talk to them. A couple of them would then try to talk to me. I was dark-skinned, but I was nobody's fool. I was not going to be a second option.

As I got older, I started to hear, "You are cute for a dark-skinned girl." Why couldn't people just say that I was a cute or pretty girl rather than point out that I was a dark-skinned girl? That was like saying that I should be grateful that I was dark-skinned *and,* according to them, cute—because many dark-skinned girls are not! So I was, again, reminded that being dark-skinned was a curse. I was talking to this guy once, and he had the nerve to tell me, "I generally don't talk to dark-skinned girls." So basically, he was telling me that I should be glad that he was giving me the time of day. And, interestingly enough, he was dark-skinned too. The nerve of him telling me that, as if he was doing me a favor. Although we both didn't realize it at the time, it was actually the other way around. The favor was on me.

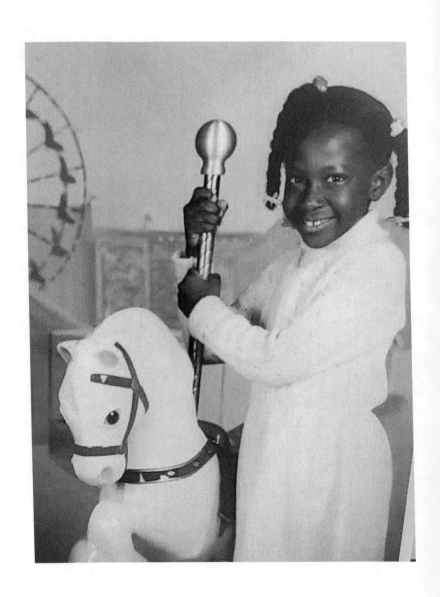

CHAPTER 4

WHEN THE FIGHTS BEGAN

As I said earlier, I grew up in a pious home, and my parents always told my siblings and me that if someone hits us we should tell an adult. They never taught us to fight. However, I was in my first fight at Margaret Willis Elementary School when I was 7 years old. I was in TK-1, which stood for transitional kindergarten. Basically, it was for students who were not ready for first grade after finishing kindergarten. This little Caucasian boy named Kevin was picking on me and calling me names on the playground. He got in my face and pushed me. I took him by his arms and swung him around and allowed him to hit the ground. All I could hear was *bloop*. Although I was only seven, I found the strength of David who had slain the lion in the Bible.

Mrs. Corn came over and asked Kevin and me what happened. Both of us started babbling at the same time. We were trying to give her our version of the story. Mrs. Corn said, "One at a time." I told her that Kevin had kept calling me names and had gotten in my face and pushed me. Kevin then gave his account. He told her that I'd started it. Mrs. Corn was Mrs. Paige's teaching assistant. She was dark-skinned, wore a jerry curl, and was about 6 feet, 4 inches tall. She took both of us to the principal's office. As we walked behind Mrs. Corn, I was in disbelief. I couldn't believe I had gotten in a fight and was on my way to the principal's office.

As I previously stated, my parents did not teach us to fight. We had been told to inform an adult.

Mrs. McRae was the principal; she was nice. But she didn't tolerate classroom disruptions and behavior problems. She was a brown-skinned, African-American lady with a slender build, who wore red lipstick and had long, red fingernails, and she always had her make-up perfectly applied on her face. She had a ruler in her hand as she spoke to us. We both thought we were going to get paddled, but we didn't. She asked us why were we in her office, and we both told her that we had been fighting. She then asked us what happened. Kevin gave his account first, and then I gave mine. She chastised both of us and told us it better not happen again. She told us that our parents sent us to school to get an education, not to act like clowns. I was relieved that she did not call our parents, because I would have surely gotten in trouble.

I didn't mention the incident on the playground to my parents, and I thought I had gotten away with it, free and clear. However, after a few months into the school year, a Parent-Teacher Conference was held. During the conference, Mrs. Corn told my mom about the fight. I remember Mrs. Corn, my mom, and I walking outside and then standing on the breezeway. Mrs. Corn said, "Mrs. Dawson, your daughter took a little boy and swung him around." My mom was appalled. But, in all honesty, I think Mrs. Corn knew I had defended myself.

Despite the fights that happened through the years, I was an exceptional student and did not cause my teachers any problems. I was part of Book It, a literacy program that awarded students who read. Once students read a book, they would get a star on their button. Once their button was filled with stars, the students would receive a certificate for a free personal pan pizza from Pizza Hut. I loved food, so I read diligently to get those free pizzas.

I not only got additional pizzas, but I also got in an additional fight. This was fight number-two.

When I was in the sixth grade, I had told my parents that I wanted to try out for the school's step team, and they told me that I could try out. I stayed after school, and after practice had ended, the coach told us to have a seat. She started talking to us about the upcoming practice. As the coach was talking, I noticed this girl named KeKe staring at me. KeKe was dark-skinned, and she lived in Melvin's Place. She was part of the Melvin's place girls posse, and no one messed with the Melvin's Place girls. They were known for fighting. I kept saying to myself, *why is she mean mugging me? What is her problem?* I tried to avoid eye-contact, but whenever I glanced in her direction, I noticed her glaring at me. I then noticed her talking to three other girls, but I couldn't really make out everything she was saying. I heard her say something about "She thinks she is all that because of her hair." I ignored her and re-directed my attention to the coach.

After the coach finished talking to us about the next practice, I gathered my belongings and headed to the parking lot to wait for my mom to arrive. The next thing I knew I felt someone attacking me from behind, and then I saw a group of girls throwing punches. Well, I wasn't going to let them beat me, so I started throwing punches too. The sad part about being jumped in this situation was that I had a cousin who was a few feet away, and she didn't even help me. Not too long after the fight had ended, I gathered my belongings, straightened my clothes out, and removed the grass out of my hair. Shortly after that, my mom came and picked me up in her brown station wagon. I didn't tell her or my dad anything. They didn't find out until months later. I didn't tell my parents because I didn't want them to come to the school. During those days, if children told their parents what was going on at school and their parent(s) came to the school, it made them look weak, and the other children would laugh and pick on them. I didn't want my parents to come to the school. If they did and someone would have said something about my parents, I would have defended them, which could have led to another fight. Plus, I was ashamed of my parents' cars. All my parents' vehicles were raggedy, except my dad's 1990 Lincoln Town Car, and he only drove it on Sundays.

My dad had an old 1972 Chevrolet truck that was white and blue, with the paint chipping, and he also had an old 1973 two-door yellow Cadillac, and only the driver's side door opened. My mom drove an old 1980-something station wagon, and the paint was chipping off that, so I did not want them coming to the school. And based on the way the school was set up, the kids could easily see all the cars pulling into the parking lot.

When I returned to school the day after the fight, there were rumors going around that I was jumped by KeKe and the Melvin's Place girls. Some of the other kids came and asked me if I had gotten jumped, and I told them I had. They would then follow-up with a foolish question: "Who won?" I simply replied, "Just know that I fought back." My blood was boiling, but I refused to allow anyone the opportunity to see that the Melvin's Place bullies had gotten the best of me. Subsequently, I never returned to step team practice again. My dreams of being on the team had been tarnished by the Melvin's Place bullies. I never even attempted to try out for the step team at Edgewood or any other school that I attended. Every time I heard about step team try-outs it invoked a memory that is forever sketched in my mind.

A few months later, I was heading to the bus right after the bell rang, which was my usual routine. Getting to the bus was a priority for me because I didn't want to miss it, nor did I want to call my mom or dad and have them pick me up. On this particular day, I walked to my bus and found a seat in the front. I always preferred to sit toward the front because there was too much going on in the back of the bus. Some of the kids had foul mouths, and some of them were being fast. While I was sitting in my seat, this brown-skinned, skinny girl with glasses named Connie came up to me and said, "You are in my seat." I replied, "What seat?" She said, "The seat that you are sitting in." I replied, "This is not your seat." She said, "Yes, it is." And I replied, "No, it is not."

Connie started fussing at me and told me I'd better get out of her seat or else. She then got in my face and launched a punch. That's when I started throwing blows, and we got in a full-blown brawl—hair pulling and all. Connie had a male cousin on the bus, and I was afraid that he would jump in the fight, but he didn't. The bus exploded in an uproar, and students gathered around to watch. The bus driver got up and pushed her way through the crowd and broke up the fight. I was sure she was going to take us to the principal, but she didn't—thank God—because both of us would have gotten suspended off the bus.

A few days later, Connie's cousin said, "Connie, I know you're my cousin, but you got your tail beat." You see, I never bothered anyone, but if someone physically attacked me, I was going to fight back. I really felt like Sofia from *The Color Purple*. In that movie, she said, "All my life I had to fight." And that year I had one fight after another. Despite the fights and the bullying, I had a successful year academically. I fought hard to maintain good grades, because I wanted to make my parents proud of me for being on the A&B honor roll. I also enjoyed attending the school awards ceremony and hearing my name called for the A&B honor roll. It gave me a sense of pride to walk across the stage and get my certificate. I walked with my head lifted high.

Reid Ross Junior High School was similar to Eastside High, the school featured in the movie *Lean on Me*. I remember kids skipping school at Reid Ross and hanging out in the woods. There were even a few students who asked me to skip school and hang with them. Skipping school was viewed as cool, but I did not want any part of it. At Reid Ross, we had our own Joe Clark as principal. His name was Mr. Robert Lucas. Mr. Lucas was an African-American, older gentlemen who had swag, a lazy eye, and one of the coolest walks ever. Mr. Lucas swung his arms whenever he walked, and when someone called his name, he would spin around on his back heels. He was an educator and disciplinarian, and he expected nothing but the best from his students and staff. He didn't take no junk and would send students to detention and suspend them if they got into a fight. Mr. Cahill was one of the assistant principals; he was more reserved, but he was stern.

There were fights all the time at Reid Ross, and speaking of fights, I was yet again in another one. This time it was with a boy named Lemuel. Lemuel was an African-American, dark-skinned guy. He sang in a group with two girls. One of the girls was named Johnetta. Lemuel thought it was cute to start picking on me and calling me Blacky, along with his other black jokes. He thought picking on me was so funny. I can see him laughing right now. I kept saying to myself, "You have some nerve calling someone Blacky when you are darker than I am."

Well, one day I'd had enough of the black jokes, and on this particular day, our teacher, Mr. Cox, had stepped out the class-room. So Lemuel got in my face. He started running his mouth and then said, "What are you going to do now?" He pushed me slightly, and it was "Murder She Wrote" from there. I pushed him back. And desks were moving and loud noises could be heard because he and I were duking it out. Mr. Cox was Caucasian and about six feet, four inches. He was one of the nicest teachers I ever had. He came back into the classroom and stopped the fight. He then escorted us to Mr. Cahill's office.

Lemuel gave his side of the story, and I gave mine. To avoid taking sides, Mr. Cahill suspended both of us for three days. Mr. Cahill called my mom, and she came to the school and talked to him. He explained to her what took place. Mr. Cox, basically told her that Lemuel had it coming because he was always picking on me. I stayed home for those three days, and my mom and dad reminded me of their rule: "If a person starts a fight with you, tell the teacher." But little did they know that they had a daughter who had become a little Joe Louis. I was tired of being bullied. But I would only fight if I was attacked. I wasn't telling no teacher. If someone hit me, my response was a hit back.

My mom and dad also told me that I was beautiful and that I should not allow others to define me with their words. Lemuel and I finished out the year without getting into any more fights, and his black jokes became fewer and far between. I had my share of fights at school, but my next fight took place in a totally different environment.

My parents started pastoring in 1991, and being a preacher's kid brought its own set of challenges. I saw my parents go through so much with people. They gave until it hurt. As I mentioned previously, my siblings and I often slept on pallets so that someone who was in need could have a soft bed to lie in. However, we were many times misunderstood, and some people disliked us for being pastors' kids. They thought we had the best life, but that was not true. Our wants were neglected at times because someone needed counseling or had a monetary need.

One Sunday afternoon my dad was a guest speaker at another church, and this girl named Chevette, who went to our church, was at this other church too. Chevette was heavy-set and light-skinned. She had a cousin named Shukney. Shukney was nice and did not mess with me. However, Chevette would always talk about me and pick on me. Well, after service, Chevette made her way to where I was and started talking junk. I do not recall what happened next, but I do know that we were on the ground. My sister was pulling me off her. Then she helped me retrieve my shoes, which had flown across the church yard. Someone ran in the church and told our parents that we were fighting. My mom immediately demanded to know what was going on, and I told her. Then she told me to get in the car. Once we were in the car, my sister explained to Mom and Dad that Chevette had started the fight.

I then received a lecture from Dad. He was famous for saying, "I cannot be teaching and preaching to other people, and my children are acting unbecoming." In my mind, I was saying *Yeah, yeah. So we're supposed to turn the other cheek? Not in my book.* I was tired of people messing with me, and as I previously stated, once I was attacked, I fought back—no questions asked. I was not going to get permission from anyone to defend myself from being physically attacked. Don't get me wrong; I suffered a lot of verbal bullying, and I took it. But when I was bullied physically, I responded physically. Sometimes you have to fight.

CHAPTER 5

HUMILIATION

The cliché "Sticks and stones may break my bones, but words will never hurt me" is one of the biggest lies that has ever been told. Words hurt, and I am a testament to that truth. The derogatory words that I heard growing up caused a mental scar that took years to heal. It caused me to devalue my self-worth and have low self-esteem. I gave off a persona that made it seem as though I was a tough person, but I was a byproduct of bullying, and those mental scars didn't heal until I was in my twenties.

The entire bullying experience spawned a plethora of feelings. I felt humiliated, ashamed, sad, ugly, and rejected. I wasn't bullied when I was alone, but I was bullied in front of my peers. My bullies needed an audience, where they could draw energy from the laughter and snickers. Some of my peers would be instigators and would say, "Are you going to let her call you that?", or "You going to let him say that to you and not do anything about it?" The instigators made those comments to provoke me to fight, but I did not allow their words to lure me into fighting. I would say to myself, *they can say whatever they want to as long as they do not put their hands on me. I am okay.* But the words were like a cancer inside me, eating away at my soul. To be belittled on a continuous basis felt like a dentist filling a cavity without numbing the tooth. It hurt. I felt ashamed to go to school sometimes because I knew that it was going to be a "roast Lenora day." There were many days when I wanted to cry, but I refused to allow my bullies to see me cry, because crying was viewed as a sign of weakness and as an indicator that they had gotten under my skin.

I once heard someone say that, when looking for employment, dark-skinned women have three strikes against them: one, they are women; two, they are African-American women; and three, they are dark-skinned woman. I got my first summer job at the age of 15 years old through the Cumberland County Workforce Development Program. Under the Workforce Development Program, I worked as an administrative assistant in the front office of Reid Ross Year-round Classical School. I answered the phones, filed papers, made copies for teachers, delivered supplies to the teachers' classrooms, and provided any additional support to the administrative staff as needed. Those I remember most were Ms. Saundra McNeil, Mrs. Pamela Marks, Ms. Carolyn Winfrey, and Mrs. Cindy McCormic. These ladies provided great mentorship for me and inspired me to be great. Ms. Saundra and Mrs. Marks both worked in the office. Mrs. Marks would always take me on errands with her. She would say, "Come on, Lenora. You can ride with me." Periodically, after work, I would hang out with her at her house and just enjoy being my authentic self. Her home was beautiful. I said to myself *when I grow-up I am going to have a beautiful home like Mrs. Marks.* She introduced me to her two daughters, her husband, her mother, and a couple of her sisters. I remember going to Spring Lake one day with her to visit her mother. Mrs. Marks was very kind, giving, and lovable.

Mrs. Cindy McCormic was the assistant principal and served under Mr. Terry Brown. Mrs. McCormic was awesome. She would say, "Lenora, have you had breakfast?" I would say, "No, ma'am." Then she would say, "Pam, take this money and go get us some breakfast from Bojangles." I was always able to get my favorite: a Cajun filet biscuit, with fries and a sweet tea. Mrs.

McCormic also introduced me to her family. I met her daughter, husband, and mother. Mrs. McCormic was the first person to take me shopping at an actual clothing store. I will never forget that day after work when she said, "Lenora, do you want to ride home with me?" I knew it would be okay with my mom because she knew Mrs. Marks, Mrs. McCormic, and Ms. McNeil and allowed me to go home with them anytime. So, I said, "Yes, ma'am." Mrs. McCormic said, "Okay. We are going to Hamricks, and I am going to take momma with us." We headed to Mrs. McCormic's beautiful home, which was in a gated community, and I had the opportunity to meet her mom. I helped her mother to the car, and we headed to Hamricks. When we arrived, Mrs. McCormic said to me, "Pick out an outfit." I was overjoyed when she told me that I could pick out an outfit for myself. I picked out a Calvin Klein shirt and a khaki skirt. I had a blast at Hamricks shopping with Mrs. McCormic.

I also had the opportunity to meet Ms. Carolyn Winfrey. Ms. Winfrey was short and petite and was one of the sweetest and prettiest teachers I've ever met. She would say to me, "Lenora, you are running that front office." She would always say something positive to me. Ms. Winfrey and I still keep in contact to this day. She is such an inspiration. Working that summer job at Reid Ross Classical School provided me with a temporary escape from the humiliation I experienced while being bullied. Working there also boosted my self-esteem.

During my junior year, at Terry Sanford High School, my business teacher, Mrs. Autry, told the class that she had a co-op opportunity available and that we needed to submit our résumés to her for consideration. She submitted my résumé, along with a few other students' résumés, for the position at Dr. Kenneth B. Lewis' dental office. I received an interview appointment. I was excited, but I was a little nervous about going in for the interview. A few days later, my teacher called me and told me that they were going to call me and offer me the job. I worked with his office until I graduated with my undergraduate degree from Fayetteville State University.

I was the only African -American working at Dr. Lewis' office, and there were times when some of the patients acted differently toward me because of my dark skin. For example, after signing her credit card receipt, a Caucasian lady chose to put the receipt on the counter rather than place it in my hand. I think she did that so she wouldn't risk touching my hand. I wanted to say, "It's not going to rub off."

Some of the White patients really didn't want me assisting them and would ask to speak to Janet, the office manager, or they preferred Tonya, the other administrative assistant, to check them out. I never said anything about it to the officer manager because I needed my job, and I knew some people were just ignorant. But I did feel rejected. Often, when people called the office to make appointments, they were so pleasant over the phone. I spoke like a professional, and they assumed talking like a professional meant the same thing as sounding White. I would tell them my name and tell them to ask for me when they arrived. And I'd tell them that I would assist them when they came in. When they'd come in, they would say, "Can I speak to Lenora?" I'd say, "I am her." Some of them would look so appalled to see that I was African-American—and a dark one at that.

My co-worker Tonya was Caucasian and had big, pretty brown eyes. She was the senior administrative assistant and had a vibrant personality. She had a beautiful soul. She kept a smile on my face often. One day she said, "Lenora, you look like Whoopi Goldberg." I immediately responded, "No, I do not." She said,

"Yes, you do. Lenora, Whoopi is pretty." I could not conceptualize that I looked like Whoopi Goldberg because the only thing I could see was Whoopi's character Celie, from *The Color Purple*. All I could hear in my head was Nathan calling me Celie, and Shug Avery's voice saying to Celie, "You sho' is ugly." Feelings of sadness and the thought of viewing myself as ugly overshadowed the compliment that Tonya was trying to get me to receive. I never told Tonya why I was so adamant about denouncing that I looked like Whoopi because I didn't have the courage to talk to her about how hearing that name opened a river of emotions.

Every time I looked in the mirror, all I saw was ugliness. My dark skin, in my eyes, was not beautiful. I didn't even like taking pictures, especially with others, because I knew that I would be the darkest person in the picture. If I had to take pictures, I would always say that I needed to make sure I was standing in the light, as if the light was going to make me lighter. I sometimes cried at night, wondering why God had made me dark. I couldn't even see that I was a reflection of my beautiful mother.

Then I started hearing the famous cliché "The blacker the berry, the sweeter the juice." But to me, that was not applicable to dark-skinned women, but rather to Black men. I remember this guy in junior high school named James. James was dark-skinned with an athletic build, and he had the prettiest white teeth. The girls used to gush over how fine James was, but I cannot recall anyone ever gushing over me. Nope, not one, and if there was, I never noticed. I just wanted to trade the shade of my blackness. Trading the shade of my blackness would have allowed me to trade the feelings that drowned me in a pit of anguish and despair.

CHAPTER 6

GOD MADE ME DARK

By the time I was in my early twenties, I finally realized there was nothing I could do about my dark skin. I embraced my darkness. I said to myself *I can't change my color, and God made me dark anyway.* I cannot wash it off, nor will I bleach it. I also realized that, if God wanted me to be another color, HE would have painted me that way. HE picked out my color prior to picking out my parents. I started telling myself, *Lenora, you are a beautiful woman. Don't allow the opinions of others to define your beauty.* I had to let go of the self-hatred that I had toward myself and love the skin I was born in. The transformation that took place in my mind was amazing. My melanin is beautiful.

MELANIN

My melanin is beautiful. I will never despise
or hide the beauty of my skin

The glow that it depicts permeates from within.

The acceptance that God the Creator made
me dark, allowed me to walk around with
confidence, like Noah after he built the ark.

There were times that I thought my darkness was a curse,
especially when the bullying went from bad to worse, but now I
see all of the name-calling and isolation was part of my destiny.

God knew that there would be other little girls and boys who would feel the same, but HE allowed me to conquer everything that I experienced so that the world would know my name.

I no longer look in the mirror, wondering if my skin color is going to change, like a person watching the stocks fluctuating on the New York Stock exchange.

I know that I am fearfully and wonderfully made, embracing everything that God created, loving that my darkness will never fade.

I will share my story worldwide, until the breath leaves my body and I close my eyes and die.

My melanin is beautiful, can't you see? God assigned my hue prior to picking out my family.

I no longer allow remarks such as, "Oh, you're cute to be a dark-skinned girl" to get to me. I know my dark skin is beautiful. Why? Because God made me unapologetically dark, and I am so confident in my skin, like a puppy belting out his first bark.

One day, as I was leaving a church I was visiting and getting in my car, a woman said to me "You are a pretty dark-skinned girl. You really don't see that often." I did not even allow her ignorant comment to ruffle my feathers. I politely said thank you, without even confronting her about the statement.

God didn't make a mistake when HE made me. HE drew me on a canvas. HE took out HIS pen and sketched my entire body structure. HE then sketched my hair, knowing how many strands HE wanted on my head and the length HE wanted my hair to be. After HE sketched my body structure, HE then took out HIS paintbrush and palette to start painting me. On HIS palette, there were several colors: white, orange, black, brown, red, blue, green, yellow, and purple. HE started first with the blue, orange, yellow, and purple and created a dark brown color. HE then got to the point where HE probably said to HIMSELF, *Should I add some white to lighten Lenora up or should I add black to give her a darker skin tone?* HE chose the latter. HE took HIS paint brush and dipped it in the black paint, and the beautiful picture on the canvas was created. I was not only a reflection of my beautiful, dark-skinned mother, but I was also a reflection of God HIMSELF.

I finally came to the realization that my dark skin is not a curse, but a blessing. Despite the challenges that I faced, I realize now that this was a journey I had to travel. There was a reason why I went through all of this: One day I would find enough strength to write about it and share my story with the world. I want to encourage all children and adults to love themselves and not allow the media or people's comments to tell them what beauty looks like.

I eradicated the mindset about limiting my options for marriage to only light-skinned men just to have light-skinned or golden-brown children. I decided I would embrace the person that God had in store for me. And guess what? God did not see fit for me to marry a light-skinned man, but HE allowed me to marry a dark-skinned man, to let me know that what I thought I wanted was not what I needed. And I must say Harold and I are a great-looking, dark-skinned couple. I love my dark-skin so much now. And if God blesses us with children, I want beautiful chocolate babies.

I MADE YOU DARK

I made you dark like your mother and like Moses' wife,
Do you remember, Lenora? She was from the Cushites.

She was picked on because of her dark skin, and I punished
Miriam and made her feel the pain from within.

I turned her skin snow white and allowed her
to see how she caused all that strife.

You may never see your bullies again, but just know, if they
read your book, they will remember where and when.

Your acceptance makes you free like a bird who can soar,
versus being in denial, causing your soul to be at war.

HE MADE HIM DARK

I had a visual image of my future husband, and
he was supposed to be fine and light,

Light so I could have some pretty brown-skinned
babies to share as the highlight of my life.

Little did I know that God had another plan, and HE
sent me a tall, dark, and handsome athletic-built man.

God knew that my request was silly,

and would have denied my request even if I
asked for my husband's name to be Billy.

God knows exactly what we need—I was
looking through the lens called vanity.

Those lenses were fogged by my own insecurities, but after
embracing everything about me represented my maturity.

I am not the only one who probably thought this way,

I am sure there are many others whose
thoughts became their biggest prey.

NO BLEACH

No bleach will ever be applied to this dark skin.

I will not mess up the complexion the Creator
designated for me before the world began.

My brothers and my sisters, I encouraged
you to put the tube down.

You are beautiful just the way you are, just like a
king and queen with or without their crown.

YOU ARE BEAUTIFUL

You are beautiful just the way God made
you, never let others tell you different.

The color of your skin, size of your eyes,
even the curve of your hips

Should always speak positive about your
beauty, from the width of your own lips.

No need for someone to validate your beauty.

Just because you don't need validation doesn't make you snooty.

The glistering of your eyes, regardless if they
are green, hazel, blue, or brown,

See your beauty as you walk past the mirror building downtown.

Darling, walk in confidence, like a horse trotting
with its head high, exuding predominance

You are beautiful, can't you see, no matter
what others think beauty should be.

KISSED BY THE SUN

I was kissed by the sun, just like my dear momma,

Sorry that it took me awhile to accept my darkness,
like watching a series of different dramas.

Momma, your milk-chocolate skin is smooth as it can be,

I couldn't see the beauty of it because of
my color blindness, but now I see.

I am glad that God made me a reflection of you,

You are a magnificent woman, and sometimes
I just look at you and say to myself, *whew!*

Whew, because, despite you telling me one
day as we were walking together,

That you wanted to bleach your beautiful black skin
as if it was easy, like dying a bird's feather.

I am glad you didn't listen to your own
thoughts or other's recommendations,

But you had enough confidence in your beauty as a
doctoral candidate defending her dissertation.

I will not hide from the Sun if it wants
to kiss me and make me darker,

I wouldn't care if I was the color of a black magic marker.

FORGIVE ME

Will YOU forgive me, God, for questioning
the pigment of my skin?

I was young. The bullying made me feel like I was in a tailspin.

At that time, I couldn't understand. It seemed
like my skin received an extra sun tan.

YOU knew the entire bullying experience
was part of my journey.

YOU knew I would come out on top
like a contestant in a tourney.

With a grateful heart, I know YOU forgave me.

Because YOU kept whispering in my ear,
"Daughter, black is how I made you."

CHAPTER 7

GREATNESS HAS NO COLOR

The color of my skin was not a problem until I was bullied about it. I was seven when my darkness was viewed as an issue. However, I now realize that the color of my skin no longer defines me. Even though I was bullied, I still dreamed of being a lawyer as far back as the fourth grade. I was bullied, but I still had dreams. Despite not becoming a lawyer, I have always desired to make a difference in the world and serve humanity. I desired a life of health, wealth, and prosperity. I am beautiful, intelligent, and lovable. I am a leader, speaker, motivator, sister, daughter, wife, confidante, author, singer, minister, and a change agent. No one, and I do mean no one, can take that away from me. I am a humble soul, but I am confident in my ability to impact the world through sharing my gifts and talents.

I am so glad I embraced everything that happened to me on this journey called life. Embracing it allowed me to conquer it, and conquering those experiences allowed me to step into my greatness. Who would have thought the young girl who contemplated slitting her wrist would materialize into this great woman? People treated me like dirt, but little did they know that they were fertilizing the leader, speaker, author, and life coach that had been planted inside of me. The tears that I cried provided the water needed to make those seeds grow within me. I want this book to be read by everyone—because everyone is battling something.

Looking back on history, Harriet Tubman, Mary McLeod Bethune, Coretta Scott King, Rosa Parks, Malcolm X, Martin Luther King, and Muhammad Ali were different shades of blackness, but their shades of blackness did not deter them from being great. Greatness truly has no color. How long will you color greatness?

At the age of 15, I was working and helping run the front office at a newly developed year-around school. I also helped my mom and sister host birthday parties for children in our neighborhood who did not have a lot. They had moved down from New Jersey and soon became part of our extended family. I also helped babysit and styled some of the little girls' hair in our neighborhood for church.

During the last couple of months of my senior year in high school, I still hadn't applied to any colleges yet. My guidance counselor, Mrs. Pamela Darden, brought me to her office and asked me which college I want to attend. I told her that I wanted to attend Bennett College or Fayetteville State University. She told me to look at the pros and cons of each. I eventually applied to Fayetteville State University and was accepted. I received an anonymous scholarship for $500, which I was so thankful for. During the first few weeks of my first semester at Fayetteville State University, I learned that I was a Chancellor Scholar and received a full scholarship.

Shortly before graduating from high school, I met with Mrs. Darden, who shared with me that someone wanted to meet me. A local general manager at a car dealership named Mr. Ruth and his wife had heard about me. They wanted me to bring my insurance card and my license to the dealership. My dad drove me to the dealership. When we arrived, I told the receptionist that I was there to see Mr. Ruth. She escorted my father and me to Mr.

Ruth's office, and there he was—a medium-built Caucasian man with glasses, sitting in his executive chair. He told my father and me to have a seat. He then told me that he had a used car that he and his wife wanted to give me. I was flabbergasted. He said my name preceded me, and he had heard a lot of great things about me. He said the only thing that they were asking of me was to keep my grades up in college. He went on to say that I should give them a call if I had any problems with the car.

The Ruths kept their word. They ensured that I had transportation until I finished school. Anytime I had an issue, I would call Mr. Ruth or stop by the dealership. I used to get tickled because, on a few occasions, when I stopped by the dealership and asked to see Mr. Ruth, some of the employees would look at me as if to say, "Who is this young lady walking in here asking for the GM?" They would call him, and he would come out and greet me with a hug. I would take them gifts around Christmastime, and they would say, "Lenora, you don't have to do this." But that was the least I could do. I will never forget the Ruths and the seeds they planted in my life.

The Ruths moved out of Fayetteville, and I lost touched with them. But I will never forget how they touched my life and poured into me. I graduated as an undergrad, debt-free. Greatness has no color.

After completing my undergraduate degree, I wanted to attend law school, but had a hard time passing the LSAT. I was heartbroken. I received rejection letter after rejection letter. The last school I applied to sent me a letter in the mail. My dad gave me the letter. After finding out that I hadn't gotten accepted, I ran to my room and cried. My dad encouraged me and told me not to feel bad about it. I spoke to my mentor at that time, Mrs. Wendy Vonnegut, a professor at Methodist College which is now Methodist University, and she encouraged me to apply to graduate school. I applied to the University of North Carolina at Pembroke and obtained a master's degree in public administration in a year and a half. I was the first person to graduate with a master's degree in my immediate family and was the first to graduate with a master's degree on my maternal grandmother's side of the family. I am also the only author in my immediate family.

My family was involved in a horrible accident in 2000, and the lawyer attempted to slight us on our compensation. Although I never went to law school, I felt compelled to conduct my own research concerning our situation. I told my family not to discuss anything with the lawyer until I presented my findings. When we did approach the lawyer with what I had discovered, he was baffled and turned red. He eventually compensated us more than he had intended to. I may not have been a lawyer, but there was still greatness inside of me.

Even though I was called "darkey," "black smut," and "Blacky Ella," I knew what name was on my birth certificate, and that name was Lenora. I never knew what my name meant, and I am not even sure if my parents knew what my name meant when they gave it to me. One day I looked up my name. Lenora means *shining light*. Even in my darkest moments, I still shined. I am like the moon lighting up the darkness of the night, and like the sun giving light during the day. I am an overcomer, and I am glad I am alive to share my story.

I made up my mind a long time ago that I will let every person I meet know that he or she is beautiful or handsome and that he or she was born to be great. I will share my greatness with the world. I will utilize all my God-given talents to help inspire, motivate, uplift, and transform the lives of others. Never allow a person to tell you that you are not pretty enough, light enough, skinny enough, or even dark or big enough. If you have some sort of disability, be grateful for the way God made you and keep in mind that we all were made in HIS image, and HIS image is magnificent. You were wonderfully made by an awesome God. And HE's always there with you through whatever it is that comes against you. Always remember, you are enough. You are smart enough, good enough, tough enough, bold enough, and beautiful enough. You are great in whatever skin you're in, because your greatness shines from within you.

GREATNESS HAS NO COLOR

Do you know that greatness has no color?

You can be great like any successful sister or brother.

The bullying could not deny the greatness and power
that I had inside, never knowing that I would be an
author, speaker, and life coach and one day experience
the serenity and joy of being a beautiful bride.

My bullies did not realize that one day
they would be part of my story.

Not for my own fame, but for God's glory.

Little did they know what the girl "Blacky,"
as they called me, had inside

Grown up to a woman filled with humble pride.

She will now motivate, inspire, and speak into the lives of
millions, gracing platforms like a debutante at her first cotillion.

PREDESTINED

Before I was born, my life was predestined like Clint
Eastwood, saving the good guy in an old country western.

God knew the path that I had to take. HE even
knew it was not going to be a piece of cake.

The time that I took the knife, contemplating slicing my wrist;
HE knew that it was part of the story that had a little twist.

HE even knew the parents of my bullies
and the bullies' full names

and knew that during a few of the fights that I
was accused and the one who was blamed.

Those fights taught me to always defend myself;
often feeling alone like the elf on the shelf.

I didn't understand why I went through so much, but now I
know why— because there are many lives that I must touch.

Letting them know that my life was predestined even before the
world began. HE even knew that I would not have many friends.

I am grateful now that HE carried me through, because HE
knew that I needed the experience so that I can pour into you.

MY DADDY NAMED ME

I asked my mommy, "Who picked out my name?" She
said, "Your daddy." I guess she did not feel like playing
the "what we're going to name this baby" guessing game.

Little did my daddy know that my name means
light, because his baby girl was going to tell others
you can make it and you will be alright.

I thought my daddy was trying to name me after
him, because his name was Leo, not realizing
that one day I would be someone's shero.

I thought he would have named me Queen, Ruby,
or Catherine, but he wanted my name to be
Lenora, oh the joy that my name would bring.

Thank you, daddy, for giving me this name. I will forever
cherish and promote love and positive change.

COLOR

Mirror, Mirror on the wall, "What color
is the prettiest of them all?"

Is it black, brown, white, beige, or cream?

Purple, blue, red, or ivory?

One color is not prettier than the other one.

They were all created equal, just like the stars, moon, and sun.

People have allowed the color of one's
skin to bring hate and divide.

When we should all be like the colors of
a rainbow and become unified

Now look in the mirror and tell me which one is prettier—

Neither of them.

Just because one is lighter than the other
does not make a person wittier.

Each color is beautiful, can't you see?

As a newborn baby wearing her first onsie.

NOTES

1 "Statistics and Laws." *Riverside Medical Clinic Charitable Foundation*, Riverside Medical Clinic Charitable Foundation, https://www.rmccharity.org/bullying-prevention-institute/resources/facts-and-laws/. Accessed 31 May 2019.

2 "Effects of Bullying." *StopBullying.gov*, U.S. Department of Health and Human Services, https://www.stopbullying.gov/at-risk/effects/index.html. Accessed 31 May 2019.

For speaking engagements, book signings,
interviews, and appearances, contact...

Lenora Lassiter

Website

www.lenoralassiter.com

E-mail

ffdarkness7@gmail.com

Facebook

facebook.com/LenoraLassiter/

Instagram

@lenoralassiter

Twitter

@lenoralassiter

53490870R00051